So Many Ways
to Get Around

A new way to explore the animal kingdom

Editorial Director
Caroline Fortin

Executive Editor
Martine Podesto

Research and Documentation
Anne-Marie Brault
Kathleen Wynd

Cover Design
Épicentre

Coordination
Lucie Mc Brearty

Page Setup
Chantal Boyer

Production Manager
Gaétan Forcillo

Executive Illustrator
Jocelyn Gardner

Illustrations
Rielle Lévesque
Raymond Martin
Claude Thivierge
Danièle Lemay
Nicholas Oroc
Jonathan Jacques
Yves Chabot
Marie-Andrée Lemieux
(Malem)
Caroline Soucy
Richard Blais (Sketch)

Translator
Gordon Martin

Copy Editing
Veronica Schami

QUÉBEC AMÉRIQUE

The art of getting from place to place

Most living beings can move from one place to another within their environment. This may seem self-evident, but without the capacity to move around, many animals would be simply unable to survive! Thanks to their legs, wings, fins, flippers and flukes, animals can escape their predators, locate food and mates, or go off in search of a nice place to live. Whether they swim, fly or climb, or move around underwater or above or below ground, and whether they travel alone or as a group, animals are perfectly equipped to confront the challenges of their environment. Their bodies allow them to make such well-orchestrated movements that they can even put on extraordinary displays of speed, endurance, efficiency and agility.

An amphibious mammal

On solid ground the hippopotamus is pretty clumsy, but in the water this big, three-ton mammal is incredibly agile! Thanks to its slightly webbed feet, this excellent swimmer appears to literally fly through the African streams and rivers, where it spends almost all of its time, shielded from the burning rays of the sun. Using its feet like a frog, it bounds forward off the bed of the waterway or walks at top speed, completely submerged.

2

common hippopotamus
Hippopotamus amphibius

An ace hoverer

This tiny, 10-centimeter-long bird can attain speeds of approximately 40 kilometers per hour, but what is most surprising is its ability to hover! Attached to its chest are very powerful muscles that drive its wings with matchless efficiency: beating over 50 times per second, they can keep the bird aloft for over four hours.

rufous hummingbird
Selasphorus rufus

Living life by leaps and bounds

Almost two meters tall, the eastern grey kangaroo moves like a spring through the forests and wooded savannahs of eastern Australia. Using its long, strong feet and the powerful muscles in its hind legs, and balancing itself with its tail, this marsupial can escape its predators by making incredible leaps over nine meters long and attain speeds of 50 kilometers per hour.

eastern grey kangaroo
Macropus giganteus

A fish out of water

Not all fish live in the water! This strange inhabitant of muddy mangrove swamps looks like an amphibian and skips along on top of the mud using its very muscular tail and pectoral fins, which become limbs on land. Although it has no lungs, the mudskipper can breathe easily because it permanently stores a small reserve of water in its gills and has highly irrigated skin that can absorb the oxygen in the air.

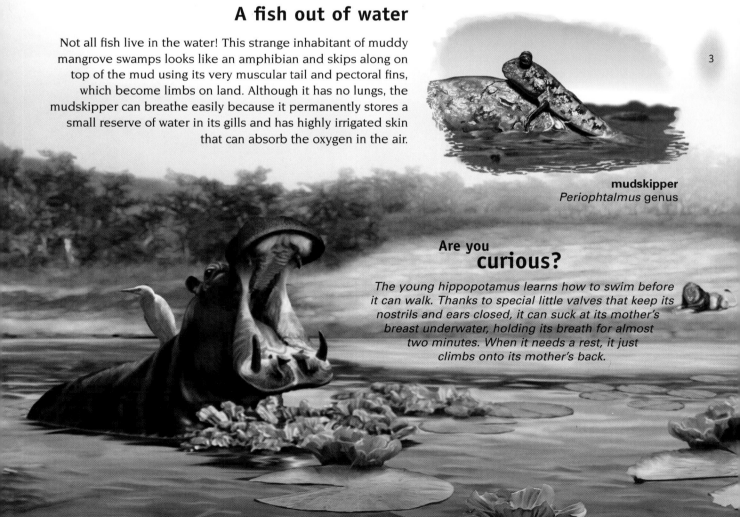

mudskipper
Periophtalmus genus

Are you curious?

The young hippopotamus learns how to swim before it can walk. Thanks to special little valves that keep its nostrils and ears closed, it can suck at its mother's breast underwater, holding its breath for almost two minutes. When it needs a rest, it just climbs onto its mother's back.

These ones are master swimmers
Olympic performances

Water is 800 times denser than air. To move around, creatures that live in the water must therefore rely on extraordinarily powerful and highly perfected tools. Master swimmers have considerable assets that allow them to live underwater. Their bodies are often streamlined to allow them to move through the water with great ease. Excellent fins that propel, steer and stabilize often assist the solid muscles responsible for the undulation of their bodies. Although fish are clearly the most efficient aquatic animals, some reptiles, birds and mammals have also chosen to spend their lives underwater.

Mammal in a diving suit

Equipped with a perfectly hydrodynamic body, fins and powerful muscles, dolphins are among the best swimmers in the seas and oceans. But the secret of their power is the special structure of the layers of their skin, which absorb the vibrations created by the currents and thwart the resistance of the water! Thanks to this incredible adaptation, these mammals attain top speeds of 65 kilometers per hour.

4

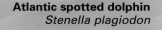

Atlantic spotted dolphin
Stenella plagiodon

The swiftness of a man-eater

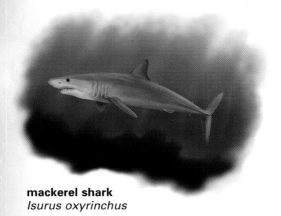

In the open waters of the Atlantic, the fearsome mackerel shark slices through the water at speeds as high as 60 kilometers per hour! With unequalled power and aggressiveness, this man-eating shark hunts down schools of mackerel and herring, or makes a mere mouthful of a swordfish without even slowing down. Famous for its phenomenal leaps, this enormous fish, which is almost four meters long, can cover up to seven meters in the air.

mackerel shark
Isurus oxyrinchus

Swimming speed record

This excellent swimmer, which can reach the incredible speed of 110 kilometers per hour, has a highly hydrodynamic body that is as streamlined as a little jet airplane! Up to six meters long, this giant of the seas has remarkable endurance that allows it to pursue schools of herring, mackerel and eels over very great distances. The swordfish not only holds speed records, it can also make spectacular leaps above the water.

swordfish
Xiphias gladius

A turtle with leathery skin

This enormous reptile, which is over two and a half meters long, is the largest living turtle and undoubtedly one of the best adapted to life in the ocean. Transformed into powerful fins, its front feet, which are incredibly broad and strong, allow it to cover 100 meters in barely 10 seconds! Known as the leatherback or leathery turtle, it has a bony shell covered with smooth skin resembling leather that allows it to glide through the water with ease.

leatherback turtle
Dermochelys coriacea

Are you curious?

In the middle of the 20th century, researchers designed a special rubber covering for submarines. Modelled on the skin of the dolphin, this "diving suit" greatly improved the performance of these underwater vessels.

These ones are master swimmers
swimming without fins

Not all aquatic animals have fins, the ideal propulsion and navigation mechanisms. But fortunately, many creatures are equipped with other means of propulsion, some of which are just as efficient as the fins of fish. Under the water, tiny single-celled animals swim by agitating thousands of cilia; snakes, eels and leeches undulate; squid propel themselves forward by releasing jets of water; and penguins swim by using their wings as fins. On the surface, insects use their feet as oars and birds row with their webbed feet.

Underwater propulsion

Thanks to its spiral shell, which is divided into about 30 little chambers filled with air and liquid, the nautilus can rise up, sink down or move forward whenever it likes. A siphon that passes through the middle of each chamber is the main component of the animal's locomotion system. By pumping water, it helps modify the balance of gases and liquids in the chambers, which allows the animal to move up and down. Furthermore, the water drawn into the siphon is forcefully pumped back out, which propels the animal around its environment.

pearly nautilus
Nautilus pompilius

Aquatic flight

Strange birds with a clumsy gait throw themselves one after another into the icy Antarctic waters. These excellent swimmers with little streamlined bodies use their rigid pinions to swim with grace and skill, reaching speeds as high as 30 kilometers per hour. On land, Adelie penguins sometimes move around by sliding along the ice on their bellies, using their feet and wings to pull themselves forward.

Adelie penguin
Pygoscelis adeliae

sea snake
Laticauda colubrina

Underwater undulations

On solid ground the sea snake, or sea krait, slithers with great skill, and underwater it swims like a champion. Using its tail, which is compressed on both sides, it paddles and undulates through the water in search of prey. Located on top of its head, its nostrils are fitted with a special valve that allows them to be closed. Although rather mild-mannered, this reptile has extremely dangerous venom that can kill human beings.

Arctic loon
Gavia arctica

Remarkable divers

Whether they dive down deep in search of food or dabble prudently on the surface, ducks and loons have the ideal equipment: large webbed feet they use as oars. A special gland at the base of their backs produces an oil that makes their feathers waterproof. A champion swimmer and diver, the Arctic loon can dive to depths of up to 70 meters and remain under the water for up to five minutes.

Are you **curious?**

Although related to octopuses and cuttlefish, this mollusc is the only cephalopod that has a shell for a home: its body is located in the first compartment of its dwelling.

These ones are
good walkers

Whether making their way over solid ground, the surface of the water or the ocean floor, walkers each have a particular style and set of equipment. Birds and humans specialize in walking on two feet, while insects wander about on six legs in a style all their own. Standing on eight legs, crustaceans stroll across the ocean floor, while starfish crawl on 1,000 little tube feet, and centipedes pace up and down on their hundreds of legs, co-ordinating their movements perfectly.

Walking on water lilies

Perched on its long legs, the jacana walks with a light step across the surface of the water, supporting itself on lotuses, water lilies and other floating aquatic plants. Acting not unlike snowshoes, its feet and disproportionately long toes, which have long, thin nails, provide perfect support for its well-distributed body weight and prevent the bird from sinking into the water. In fact, the limbs of the jacana are so well adapted for walking on water that the bird has trouble getting around on land.

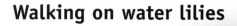

8

African jacana
Actophilornis africana

Insects on skates

With each step, the water strider glides gracefully for several centimeters across the surface of the water, without ever sinking. While its short front legs are busy capturing prey, its middle ones row to propel the insect forward, assisted by its hind legs, which serve as rudder. A clump of hairs under the body of the strider traps air and prevents the insect from getting wet!

water strider
Gerris paludum

The great sea walker

A member of the spider-crab family, this animal has extraordinarily long legs that are specially designed to allow it to move around on the muddy floors of the deepest seas. With a body that measures 30 centimeters in diameter, it is the largest crustacean in the world. When fully extended, its legs span a little over three meters!

giant crab
Macrocheira kaempferi

Feet, feet and more feet...

Contrary to what their name suggests, no millipede actually has 1,000 feet. In fact, most of the approximately 8,000 species have fewer than 200! Slowly snaking their way through damp soil and rotting vegetation, julids have their own special way of getting around: they move all the legs on one side of their body almost simultaneously, with a slight delay between each successive forward leg and the one immediately behind it. This unusual way of walking creates the illusion of a wave passing through the entire length of the insect's body..

Julid
Lulidae family

Are you curious?

The nest of the jacana is a remarkably simple structure: made from the stems of water lilies, leaves and reeds, it rests on floating plants. The jacana's four eggs have a lustre that protects them from the water.

Some animals are
excellent acrobats

Performing numerous acrobatic feats and high-flying stunts, squirrels and monkeys leap from branch to branch. Woodpeckers, tree creepers, dormice and martens climb tree trunks with extraordinary skill, while flies and lizards move around on ceilings with disconcerting ease, with their heads resting on nothing but air! These incredible acrobats have all the equipment they need to perform spectacular maneuvers: many of them have light, supple bodies, as well as powerful legs and claws that support their body weight and defy gravity. Furthermore, some of these animals also have prehensile tails, which become a fifth limb whenever necessary.

A domestic companion

It is hard to believe that a large, 35-centimeter-long lizard can climb up and down the walls, and even walk on the ceilings, of the homes it chooses to inhabit. But the tokay gecko skilfully performs this maneuver using the long digits and sharp claws on its feet. Its secret? Under each digit is a series of treads fitted with thousands of microscopic bristles that act as suckers and allow the lizard to cling to almost any smooth surface!

Are you curious?

This lizard, which makes a sound not unlike the bark of a dog, likes living with humans. When heard in a house, its characteristic cry is regarded as a sign of happiness.

tokay gecko
Gekko gecko

A very practical limb

To accomplish their climbing feats, arboreal animals like spider monkeys and opossums use their tail as if it were another arm or leg. Very practical, the muscular tail of the tree porcupine coils itself firmly around the branches, which allows it to climb with complete peace of mind in search of the leaves, stems and fruit it feeds on when night falls.

prehensile-tailed porcupine
Coëndou prehensilis

The acrobat of the tropical forests

Gibbons are ace acrobats! Using their very flexible, muscular and, most importantly, disproportionately long arms, they swing spectacularly, diving from branch to branch in the summits of tall trees in tropical forests. These masters of the means of locomotion known as "brachiation" can leap through the air 10 meters at a time, reaching speeds of over 30 kilometers per hour!

white-handed gibbon
Hylobates lar

11

A champion climber

On the trunk of a large tree, the Eurasian nuthatch perches, descends headfirst and hops to one side, in search of the insects, seeds and nuts on which it feeds. These light, sparrow-sized birds have long, strong toes with sturdy nails that sink firmly into the bark of trees. Equally at ease with its head in the air or upside down, these strange little acrobats sleep with their heads lowered and tucked into a crack in the bark of a tree!

Eurasian nuthatch
Sitta europæa

While others are the masters of the sky
formidable fliers

We often think of flying as just another way of getting around. But bear in mind that 9,000 species of birds, 950 species of bats and almost a million species of insects have acquired a remarkable invention – wings. Whether short or long, thin or wide, whether designed for the take-offs of grouse, the rapid flights of falcons, the endurance flights of terns or the stationary flights of hummingbirds, whether used to glide like gulls and vultures or to perform the complicated maneuvers of swifts, wings are all marvellously adapted to the flying conditions encountered by their owners.

Gliding with genius

Taking full advantage of the air currents, whirlwinds and strong gusts over the Atlantic Ocean, the majestic wandering albatross swoops upward, downward and in a zigzag pattern, travelling up to 100 kilometers without flapping its wings even once! With its long, narrow wings that can span up to three and a half meters, the wandering albatross is one of the largest birds capable of flight.

wandering albatross
Diomedea exulans

Aerial maneuvers

Slender and delicate, dragonflies are among the fastest of all insects. Equipped with two pairs of rigid wings crossed by network of thin veins, these insects are strong fliers that can cover great distances and attain speeds as high as 75 kilometers per hour! Aerial maneuvers hold no secrets for dragonflies, which are capable of flying backward, hovering in one place or even flying straight up, like a little helicopter.

dragonfly
Libellulidae family

A tireless flier

No bird spends more time in the air than the common swift! It feeds, cleans itself, reproduces, gathers all the material required to build its nest and even sleeps at altitudes of several hundred kilometers, without ever touching down on solid ground! To take a well-deserved rest, this little 16-centimeter-long bird lands on vertical surface, clinging to it with the sturdy claws of its short legs.

common swift
Apus apus

13

Flying mammals

Chiroptera, the name of the order to which bats belong, means "wing made from a hand." But bat wings, whose shape varies from species to species, are in fact made from a thin membrane of skin that stretches from the shoulder and is supported by the arm, the forearm and five very long fingers. These little aerial acrobats are the only mammals capable of actual flight, and they can reach speeds of up to 50 kilometers per hour.

spear-nosed bat
Phyllostomatidae family

Are you curious?

Some sailors see the albatross as a sign that bad weather and storms are coming. Others believe that the bird may be the reincarnation of sailors lost at sea.

While others are masters of the sky
funny birds

Although they are the undisputed masters of the sky, insects, birds and bats share their aerial habitat with a few arboreal species that have expertise in leaping and gliding. Deploying special membranes like little parachutes, these creatures throw themselves into empty space to travel from branch to branch or to flee their enemies, sometimes covering impressive distances!

An arboreal kite

Malayan flying lemur
Cynocephalus variegatus

This elegant, cat-sized parachutist moves nimbly from branch to branch, using a membrane of skin known as the patagium, which stretches from the neck to the tail on each side of its body. This incredible adaptation allows the flying lemur to avoid travelling on the ground and solve the problem of getting from one tree to another: when gliding, it steers by varying the position of its feet and tail. The longest lemur glide ever observed measured 136 meters!

Travelling at the end of a thread

Suspended between earth and sky, the red-spotted spider crab allows itself to be carried by the wind, hanging from a long thread of silk secreted by its own spinning tubes. Held aloft by warm air currents, this practically invisible thread lifts the spider and carries it very great distances, at the speed of the wind. But when the temperature drops suddenly, the spider is forced to land and abandon this means of transportation. Once on the ground, these insects can walk both backward and sideways, which is why they are referred to as "crab spiders."

red-spotted crab spider
Misumena vatia

A lizard with wings

flying dragon
Draco genus

These little reptiles, which are about 20 centimeters long, have nothing in common with the imaginary creatures whose name they share, except perhaps their ability to fly through the air. Inhabitants of the tops of tall trees, flying dragons get from place to place by leaping and gliding through the air, five or six meters at a time. Supported by their uppermost, mobile ribs, two large lobes of skin attached along the sides of their bodies act as wings, allowing these insectivores to glide up to 60 meters through the air.

Flying like a fish

Barely six centimeters long, this little inhabitant of the rivers, swamps and ditches of Latin America uses pectoral fins that have developed into powerful muscles to skilfully leap above the water and glide to evade its enemies. By flapping its fins like wings, the hatchetfish can travel above the water for several meters!

common hatchetfish
Gasteropelecus sternicla

Are you curious?

The young flying lemur, which is born after just 60 days of embryonic life, is carried around on its mother's belly for quite some time. When she wants to glide, the mother folds over a portion of her patagium near the tail, creating a snug hammock for her little one.

These ones are champion jumpers

What do fleas, grasshoppers, pumas, deer, giant kangaroos, weasels and frogs have in common? They are all great jumpers that can cover staggering distances in a matter of seconds. Whether leaping to escape an enemy, hunt prey or just get around, these crafty creatures have a considerable advantage: the incredible spring in their step makes them much faster than walkers and leaves them much less tired than runners. From the disproportionately long and strong muscles of frogs to the efficient, highly elastic muscles that catapult insects through the air, or the supple, elongated bodies of the big cats – all these physical assets allow jumping animals to perform astounding feats.

A long-jump champion

Using its long tail to maintain its balance, the snow leopard, which is also known as the "ounce," climbs agilely along a branch. From this high, solitary perch, it waits and watches for its future meal: a wild boar, a deer, a sheep or an imprudent goat. Suddenly, like a flash of lightning, the powerful, agile animal leaps, covering no less than 15 meters in a single bound! Its body is more elongated and set lower on its legs than that of the panther, making the ounce the best jumper in the *Felidae* family.

snow leopard
Uncia uncia

The power and elegance of a giant

killer whale
Orcinus orca

With a body 10 meters long and a dorsal fin almost two meters high, the killer whale is the largest and swiftest member of the dolphin family. Forcefully projecting its enormous, 7-ton body out of the water, this giant of the seas can leap 10 meters into the air! Extraordinarily talented, this mild-mannered, highly intelligent carnivore is one of the stars of many of the aquatic shows presented around the world.

Prairie and field hopper

No great shakes as a walker or runner, this four-centimeter-long insect is never going to win any races and is also a clumsy flier. But its particularly long, third pair of legs have powerful thighs and elongated "feet" that are perfect for jumping. Using a mechanism that works like a catapult, the great green bush-cricket can make incredible leaps measuring 75 times its body length!

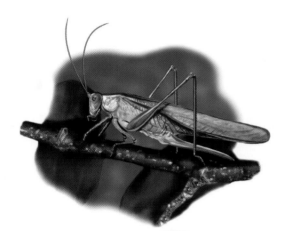

great green bush-cricket
Tettigonia viridissima

Jumping jerboas!

desert jerboa
Jaculus jaculus

Like a spring, the little desert jerboa jumps at top speed, fleeing the predators of the deserts of North Africa and the Middle East. These strange creatures, which look like miniature kangaroos, can make leaps four meters long and reach the incredible speed of 25 kilometers per hour! Veritable jumping machines, these mammals are equipped with hind legs four times longer than their front ones and a very long tail that acts as a support, a rudder and a balancing pole during jumps.

Are you curious?

Although illegal in many countries, the trade in snow-leopard fur continues and threatens the species with extinction. It is estimated that there are only 750 snow leopards left in the world.

While these ones are
champion runners

Equipped with long, thin, muscular legs and with feet designed specifically for walking on the flat ground of steppes, prairies and deserts, the great runners of the animal world have an important advantage – their speed. Whether they run on four feet like lions, gazelles or African hunting dogs or on two feet like ostriches, whether fleeing a predator or pursuing prey over great distances, and whether they are sprinters or long-distance runners, these champions run spectacular races and often emerge victorious.

A master sprinter

Thanks to its supple spine, which stretches like an accordion, its powerful back and leg muscles and its long claws, which firmly grip the ground with each stride, the cheetah is the fastest animal on earth. With its thin and elastic body, this graceful feline performs extraordinary feats: it can accelerate to speeds of 75 kilometers per hour in just two seconds and can attain top speeds of over 110 kilometers per hour!

cheetah
Acinonyx jubatus

Cool running

This reptile, which is 60 centimeters long including its tail, skilfully co-ordinates the movements of its four legs when running between desert rocks and climbing trees. However, when threatened by a predator, it stands up on its hind legs and runs away, using its long tail as a balancing pole. But that's not the only reason it runs in this ingenious fashion: the air displaced by its erect body cools the lizard off in hot weather.

bearded dragon
Amphibolurus barbatus

greater roadrunner
Geococcyx californianus

The American desert roadrunner

The greater roadrunner is certainly the most famous running bird of all! Seeming to barely make contact with the ground of the American deserts it calls home, it can reach the incredible speed of 40 kilometers per hour! Although it rarely uses its short wings to fly, they play an essential role when it runs: used in combination with the tail, they help the bird maintain its balance during its wild jaunts through the desert. Its exceptional speed allows the roadrunner to hunt its prey and protect itself from danger.

Running on hoof-tips

Famous for its gallop, this animal runs on the tips of its hooves. Each of its hooves is in fact the oversized, sturdy nail of the only one of its toes that touches the ground. Equipped with this solid protection as well as long feet and a muscular body, this horse is one of the best runners in the entire animal world. The last of the wild horses, the Przewalski now lives only in captivity. There are approximately 1,000 of them in various zoos throughout the world.

Przewalski's horse
Equus Przewalskii

Are you curious?

Although it is a champion starter, accelerator and short-distance sprinter, the cheetah is a big loser when it comes to endurance. After pursuing prey for barely 20 seconds, the cheetah has expended so much energy that it has to stop for a rest. That's why its stomach remains empty three quarters of the time.

These ones are
highly skilled surveyors

These animals know every inch of the ground by heart. Sliding and crawling on its surface or slipping into its deepest layers, they explore even the tiniest crevices, and every portion of their bodies is in constant contact with the ground. These crawling experts have no feet, but that's no problem at all! The creeping movements of flatworms, the accordion-like movements of earthworms, snails and leeches and the sinuous movements of snakes are all examples of the simple contractions of the body that allow numerous animals to move around.

Sinuous movements

The animals we now know as snakes are the descendants of four-footed reptiles. Although these much-feared animals have lost their limbs, they are no less agile than their ancestors! The black mamba, which is three meters long, is the fastest snake in the world! Undulating and insinuating its way between the plant stems and stones of dry savannahs, this extremely skilful reptile can slither at speeds of up to 20 kilometers per hour.

20

black mamba
Dendroaspis polylepis

As slow as a snail

This inhabitant of European gardens moves with legendary slowness. A wave of slight muscular contractions runs through its body, which advances on a carpet of mucus secreted by the snail itself. This substance plays a very unique role: underneath the immobile parts of the snail's foot, the mucus "sticks" to the ground to provide support. But when the foot begins to move, the mucus becomes liquid and allows the animal to glide at a speed of 40 meters per hour.

five-banded snail
Cepaea hortensis

Indispensable plows

These little creatures, which play a crucial role in maintaining healthy soil, swallow earth as they move around, thus creating countless air tunnels. The earthworm, which is present in almost all types of terrain, crawls at a speed of 30 centimeters per minute, by alternately elongating and shortening its various segments using two series of special muscles that encircle and run along its body.

earthworm
Lumbricus terrestris

Moving like an accordion

This European leech measures approximately 10 centimeters, but as it moves forward, its body stretches to twice its original length. At each tip of its body, the leech has a sucker. To advance, it attaches the rear sucker to the ground then stretches the front portion of its body like an accordion and attaches its front sucker further ahead. Its rear sucker then moves up next to the front one, and the leech repeats this maneuver until it arrives at its destination.

medical leech
Hirudo medicinalis

Are you curious?

When they undulate, snakes use the relief of their environment as well as plants and stones as supports, so they can move rapidly without rolling over onto their backs.

These ones embark
on long trips

By sea, land or air, millions of animal species embark on long migrations. These sometimes spectacular movements are often linked to factors such as climate changes, food shortages and the need to reproduce. Migrations can be one-way or return trips ranging from a few kilometers to several thousand kilometers, and the routes are often studded with obstacles. Great travellers, the animals that cover considerable distances during migrations put all their senses on the alert: to get to their destination and back, many of them rely on their hearing or their sense of smell, while others use visual markers or are guided by the earth's magnetic field or the position of the sun and stars.

Great travellers

Following trails blazed by their ancestors over thousands of years, the blue wildebeests of Serengeti National Park in Tanzania leave the southern plans to embark on an annual migration 1,500 kilometers long. Entire herds of male, female and young wildebeests in search of water and fresh pasture form a tidal wave that sweeps onto the relatively humid northern prairies. During this dangerous journey, several animals are trampled to death, drown or are eaten by hyenas and lions.

blue wildebeest
Connochætes taurinus

Criss-crossing North America

Monarch butterflies rest in a group on the trunk of a tree in eastern North America, and their thousands of colorful wings create a magnificent spectacle. In September, they leave their feeding grounds in the north to return to their winter homes in Mexico, Florida and California. The following spring, a new population of monarchs heads back up to the prairies and fields of the north, covering a distance of 2,000 to 3,000 kilometers without stopping for food or water or to rest for the night.

monarch butterfly
Danaus plexippus

Journey to the ends of the earth

In the animal world, the distance record for migrations is held by the Arctic tern. This great traveller, which is 35 centimeters long, leaves its breeding grounds in the Arctic seas to embark on an annual migration of 35,000 kilometers! Its destination is the Antarctic ice pack. This incredible journey allows the tern to enjoy the best of both Poles!

Arctic tern
Sterna paradisaea

23

The trip of a lifetime

Few fish have a life as hectic as that of the European eel. On the day they are born, the tiny larvae embark on a long and tiring 6,000-kilometer trip between the salty waters of the Sargasso Sea, their place of birth, and the fresh waters of distant rivers. When they reach adulthood 20 years later, they make the return trip to reproduce in the warm waters where they were born.

European eel
Anguilla anguilla

Are you curious?

Wildebeest societies are made up of harems. During the mating season, the harem of a single male can include as many as 150 females. To encourage the females to remain in the group, the male provides them with protection against other males and, more importantly, against predators.

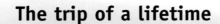

While others are condemned
to a life of immobility...

Not all animal species are mobile. On the contrary, some of them lead stationary lives. Completely immobile, these creatures are born, grow old and die in exactly the same place. To compensate for this enforced immobility, some of these animals have adapted in highly ingenious ways.

A stationary colony

Colonial corals, which build reefs in tropical seas, have rigid limestone bodies that are firmly attached to the skeletons of the corals that lived before them. Condemned to a life of immobility, they have developed a very effective feeding method: they are equipped with stinging cells known as cnidoblasts, which paralyze and capture any prey that venture near. These ingenious little creatures also live in close association with zooxanthellae, algae that transform sunlight into various nutrients corals can feed on.

coral
Hexacorallia subclass

A stationary life

Freshly hatched, the female larva of the scale insect runs up and down the stem of the plant on which it is born looking for the ideal place to settle down forever. When it finds the right spot, it attaches itself to the plant and undergoes an incredible transformation: without legs, wings or eyes and with tiny antennae, the adult female of this species looks nothing like the insect it is! Incapable of even the slightest movement, scale insects spend their entire lives attached to the same plant and feed on its sap.

scale insect
Parthenolecanium corni

An animal with panache

Under no circumstances should you attempt to pick this flower! At the first sign of danger, the magnificent crown disappears inside a limestone sheath. This beautiful plume is in fact a polychaete worm that lives inside a fixed tube. Consisting of tentacles adorned with tiny cilia, the crown of the fanworm makes up for the enforced immobility of its owner: by fluttering the millions of cilia on its tentacles, the animal attracts food toward its mouth.

fanworm
Spirographis spallanzani

25

A sedentary crustacean

This strange animal spends all of its adult life in the same position, attached to a peduncle approximately 10 centimeters long. Although sedentary, this ingenious crustacean attaches itself to a floating object, such as a piece of wood, a buoy or a bottle, thus travelling impressive distances! Using its feet, which have been transformed into little flexible organs known as "cirri," the goose barnacle filters tiny animals out of the seawater or grabs prey that happen to venture within reach.

common goose barnacle
Lepas anatifera

Are you curious?

The word "coral" comes from the Greek word "korallion," which means "sea shrub." Since Ancient times, these underwater animals have been "harvested" to make jewellery and ornaments or to prepare potions with magic properties.

1. **Hippopotamus (p. 2)**
   (sub-Saharan Africa)

2. **Rufous hummingbird (p. 3)**
   (northwestern North America, coast of the Gulf
   of California, southern California, Mexico)

3. **Eastern grey kangaroo (p. 3)**
   (eastern Australia)

4. **Mudskipper (p. 3)**
   (Africa, southeastern Asia, Oceania and
   northern Australia)

5. **Atlantic spotted dolphin (p. 4)**
   (Atlantic Ocean, tropical and temperate zones,
   Gulf of Mexico)

6. **Mackerel shark (p. 5)**
   (Atlantic Ocean)

7. **Swordfish (p. 5)**
   (all seas and ocean)

8. **Leatherback turtle (p. 5)**
   (tropical seas, often temperate and subarctic)

9. **Pearly nautilus (p. 6)**
   (Indian and Pacific Oceans)

10. **Sea snake (p. 7)**
    (coastal regions, from India to Oceania and
    from southern Japan to New Zealand)

11. **Arctic loon (p. 7)**
    (North America, from Alaska to Hudson's Bay,
    coastal regions of the Pacific Ocean)

12. **Adelie penguin (p. 7)**
    (Antarctica and the surrounding islands)

13. **African jacana (p. 8)**
    (sub-Saharan Africa)

14. **Water strider (p. 9)**
    (Palearctic region and a fraction of the oriental
    region)

15. **Giant crab (p. 9)**
    (Japan)

16. **Julid (p. 9)**
    (the Lulidae family is present on all continents)

17. **Tokay gecko (p. 10)**
    (India, Pakistan, southern China, Indochina,
    the Philippines and Indonesia)

18. **Prehensile-tailed porcupine (p. 11)**
    (Bolivia, Brazil, Guyana, Venezuela, Trinidad)

19. **White-handed gibbon (p. 11)**
    (Thailand, Malay Peninsula, northern Sumatra)

20. **Eurasian nuthatch (p. 11)**
    (Europe, Asia, northwestern Africa)

21. **Wandering albatross (p. 12)**
    (Antarctic islands and coastal regions of
    the southern continents)

22. **Dragonfly (p. 13)**
    (all countries)

23. **Common swift (p. 13)**
    (Europe, Asia, Africa)

24. **Spear-nosed bat (p. 13)**
    (Mexico, Central America, South America and
    the West Indies)

25. **Malayan flying lemur (p. 14)**
(southeastern Asia, from Burma to Borneo)

26. **Red-spotted crab spider (p. 15)**
(southern Canada, the United States, Europe)

27. **Flying dragon (p. 15)**
(southern India, China, Indonesia, the Philippines, Malaysia)

28. **Common hatchetfish (p. 15)**
(northern Latin America)

29. **Snow leopard (p. 16)**
(Pakistan, from northern Afghanistan to Siberia, from the Himalayas to China)

30. **Killer whale (p. 17)**
(all oceans and seas, from the Equator to the poles)

31. **Great green bush-cricket (p. 17)**
(western Europe, northern Africa and Asia)

32. **Desert jerboa (p. 17)**
(northern Africa and the Middle East)

33. **Cheetah (p. 18)**
(Africa, as far east as Asia)

34. **Bearded dragon (p. 19)**
(Australia, except the far north)

35. **Greater roadrunner (p. 19)**
(southwestern United States, as far as Louisiana, and Mexico)

36. **Przewalski horse (p. 19)**
(Mongolia and western China)

37. **Black mamba (p. 20)**
(from Senegal in the west to Kenya in the east and as far as southern Africa)

38. **Five-banded snail (p. 21)**
(Europe)

39. **Earthworm (p. 21)**
(Europe, North America)

40. **Medical leech (p. 21)**
(Europe)

41. **Blue wildebeest (p. 22)**
(eastern and southern Africa)

42. **Monarch butterfly (p. 23)**
(southern Canada, the United States and Mexico)

43. **Arctic tern (p. 23)**
(nests at the level of the Arctic Circle, winters in Antarctica)

44. **European eel (p. 23)**
(Atlantic Ocean, Mediterranean Sea and the North Sea, fresh waters of Europe and North Africa)

45. **Coral (p. 24)**
(all seas and oceans)

46. **Scale insect (p. 25)**
(all continents)

47. **Fanworm (p. 25)**
(Mediterranean Sea)

48. **Common goose barnacle (p. 25)**
(all oceans)

More clues for
the most curious

THE GREAT ANIMAL PERFORMANCES		
	Running champions	**...and their speed (kilometers per hour)**
	Cheetah *(Acinonyx jubatus)*	110
	Lion *(Panthero leo)*	80
	Springbok antelope *(Antidorcas marsupialis)*	80
	Red deer *(Cervus elaphus)*	78
	Domestic horse *(Equus caballus)*	70
	Emu *(Dromaius novaehollandiae)*	64
	Greyhound *(Canis familiaris)*	60
	Black rhinoceros *(Diceros bicornis)*	51
	Giraffe *(Giraffa camelopardalis)*	51
	Ostrich *(Struthio camelus)*	50
	Timber wolf *(Canis lupus)*	45
	Black mamba *(Dendroaspis polylepis)*	24
	Grey monitor *(Varanus griseus)*	22.5
	Flying aces	**...and their speed (kilometers per hour)**
In a straight line	Peregrine falcon *(Falco peregrinus)*	180
	White-throated needletail *(Chaetura pelagica)*	170
	Homing pigeon *(Ectopistes migratorius)*	151
	Spur-winged goose *(Plectropterus gambiensis)*	142
	Green-winged teal *(Anas crecca)*	120
	Hawk *(Accipiter* genus)	110
	Tundra swan *(Cygnus columbianus bewickii)*	107
	Eurasian oystercatcher *(Haematopus ostralegus)*	100
	Whooper swan *(Cygnus cygnus)*	93
	Willow ptarmigan *(Lagopus lagopus)*	90
	Dragonfly *(Odonata* order)	75
In a nosedive	Peregrine falcon *(Falco peregrinus)*	324
	Golden eagle *(Aquila chrysaetos)*	300
	Great swimmers	**...and their speed (kilometers per hour)**
	Swordfish *(Xiphias gladius)*	110
	Marlin *(Istiophoridae)*	80
	Blue shark *(Prionace glauca)*	70
	Bluefin tuna *(Thunnus thynnus)*	70
	Killer whale *(Orcinus orca)*	64
	Common dolphin *(Delphinus delphis)*	60
	Fin whale *(Balaenoptera physalus)*	48
	California sea lion *(Zalophus californianus)*	40
	Gentoo penguin *(Pygoscelis papua)*	40
	Leatherback turtle *(Dermochelys coriacea)*	35

	Great jumpers	...and their performances (kilometers per hour)
High-jumpers	Mackerel shark *(Isurus oxyrhynchus)*	7.6
	Dolphin *(Delphinidae* family*)*	7
	Killer whale *(Orcinus orca)*	6
	Leopard *(Panthera pardus)*	5.5
	Ibex *(Capra ibex)*	4.5
	Giant kangaroo *(Macropus giganteus)*	4
	Tiger *(Panthera tigris)*	4
	Chamois *(Rupicapra rupicapra)*	3.6
	Atlantic salmon *(Salmo salar)*	3.5
	Domestic dog *(Canis familiaris)*	3.5
	Impala *(Aepyceros melampus)*	3
	Domestic horse *(Equus caballus)*	2.5
Long-jumpers	Snow leopard *(Panthera uncia)*	15
	Springbok antelope *(Antidorcas marsupialis)*	15
	Giant kangaroo *(Macropus giganteus)*	13.5
	White-tailed deer *(Odocoileus virginianus)*	12.2
	Impala *(Aepyceras melampus)*	12
	Domestic horse *(Equus caballus)*	11.9
	Killer whale *(Orcinus orca)*	10
	Domestic dog *(Canis familiaris)*	9
	Springhare *(Pedetes capensis)*	9
	Chamois *(Rupicapra rupicapra)*	7.7
	Giant squirrel *(Ratufa macroura)*	6
	Frog *(Amphibia* class*)*	5
	Grasshopper *(Orthoptera* order*)*	3
	Flea *(Siphonaptera* order*)*	0.33

	Skilful divers	...and their performances (meters)
	Sperm whale *(Physeter catodon)*	3,000
	Sea elephant *(Mirounga* genus*)*	1,250
	Baird's beaked whale *(Berardius bairdi)*	900
	Weddell seal *(Leptonychotes weddelli)*	600
	Fin whale *(Balaenoptera physalus)*	500
	Emperor penguin *(Aptenodytes forsteri)*	265
	Adelie penguin *(Pygoscelis adeliae)*	70
	Diver *(Gaviidae* family*)*	55

	World-class slowpokes	...and their speed
	Dwarf sea horse *(Hippocampus zozterae)*	62 hours to cover 1 kilometer
	Brown snail *(Helix aspersa)*	25 hours to cover 1 kilometer
	Three-toed sloth *(Bradypus tridactylus)*	24 hours to cover 1 kilometer
	Galapagos tortoise *(Testudo elephantopus)*	3 hours to cover 1 kilometer

hippopotamus
Hippopotamus amphibius

class Mammals
order Artiodactylae
family Hippopotamidae

size and weight	2.8 to 4.2 m long; height at withers: 1.3 to 1.65 m 1.3 to 3.2 tons
distribution	sub-Saharan Africa
habitat	lakes, rivers
diet	grasses
reproduction	1 baby; 24-day gestation period
predators	humans, lions
life span	45 years (in captivity)

Atlantic spotted dolphin
Stenella plagiodon

class Mammals
order Cetacea
family Delphinidae

size and weight	2 to 2.7 m 110 to 145 kg
distribution	Atlantic Ocean, tropical and temperate zones of the Gulf of Mexico
habitat	coastal regions
diet	fish, cephalopods
reproduction	1 baby; 11-month gestation period

pearly nautilus
Nautilus pompilius

class Cephalopods
order Tetrabranchiata
family Nautilidae

size	15 to 20 cm long
distribution	Indian and Pacific Oceans
habitat	depths of 50 to 100 m
diet	crustaceans, fish

African jacana
Actophilornis africana

class Birds
order Charadriiformes
family Jacanidae

size	22 to 28 cm
distribution	sub-Saharan Africa
habitat	lakes, rivers, swamps, slow-moving waterways
diet	insects, molluscs, small fish, seeds
reproduction	4 to 6 eggs (up to four clutches per season); 22- to 24-day incubation period

tokay gecko
Gekko gecko

class Reptiles
order Squamata
family Gekkonidae

size	28 to 35 cm
distribution	India, Pakistan, southern China, Indochina, Philippines and Indonesia
habitat	trees, rocks, human dwellings
diet	spiders, insects, small lizards and young rodents
reproduction	1 to 2 eggs (4 to 6 clutches per year); 120- to 140-day incubation period

wandering albatross
Diomedea exulans

class Birds
order Procellariiformes
family Diomedeidae

size	1 m long; wingspan: 3 to 3.5 m
distribution	Antarctic islands and the coastal regions of the southern continents
habitat	ocean
diet	cephalopods, fish, crustaceans and refuse from ships
reproduction	1 to 2 eggs every 2 years; 70- to 80-day incubation period
life span	30 years

Malayan flying lemur
Cynocephalus variegatus

class Mammals
order Dermoptera
family Cynocephalidae

size and weight	33 to 42 cm long; tail: 22 to 27 cm 1 to 1.75 kg
distribution	south-eastern Asia, from Burma to Borneo
habitat	forests, plantations, plains
diet	shoots, buds, flowers, fruit, leaves
reproduction	1 baby; 60-day gestation period
predators	Philippine eagle, humans
life span	unknown

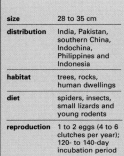

snow leopard
Uncia uncia

class Mammals
order Carnivora
family Felidae

size and weight	1 to 1.5 m long; tail: 70 cm to 1 m 25 to 70 kg
distribution	Pakistan, from northern Afghanistan to Siberia, east of the Himalayas as far as China
habitat	alpine prairies, mountain slopes, forests
diet	mice, marmots, hares, wild boars, sheep, goats and birds
reproduction	2 to 5 young; 90- to 103-day gestation period
life span	16 to 18 years (in captivity)

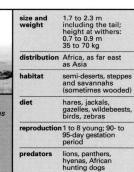

cheetah
Acinonyx jubatus

class Mammals
order Carnivora
family Felidae

size and weight	1.7 to 2.3 m including the tail; height at withers: 0.7 to 0.9 m 35 to 70 kg
distribution	Africa, as far east as Asia
habitat	semi-deserts, steppes and savannahs (sometimes wooded)
diet	hares, jackals, gazelles, wildebeests, birds, zebras
reproduction	1 to 8 young; 90- to 95-day gestation period
predators	lions, panthers, hyenas, African hunting dogs
life span	20 years (in captivity)

black mamba
Dendroaspis polylepis

class Reptiles
order Squamata
family Elapidae

size and weight	an average of 3 m long
distribution	from Senegal in the west to Kenya in the east and as far as southern Africa
habitat	savannahs and dry tropical forests
diet	birds and small mammals
reproduction	9 to 14 eggs
predators	eagles

blue wildebeest
Connochætes taurinus

class Mammals
order Artiodactylae
family Bovidae

size and weight	2.3 to 3.4 m long including the tail 140 to 260 kg
distribution	eastern and southern Africa
habitat	savannahs, steppes, sparse forests
diet	young grass shoots
reproduction	1 baby; 8- to 9-month gestation period
predators	lions, spotted hyenas, leopards, cheetahs, crocodiles, jackals, African hunting dogs
life span	18 to 20 years

coral
Hexacorallia subclass

class Anthozoans
order 7 different orders of coral

distribution	all seas and oceans
habitat	lagoons, abyssal depths, tropical, temperate and cold waters
diet	aquatic larvae, fish eggs, tiny crustaceans, little worms
predators	parrotfish, marine gastropods, worms, crustaceans, boxfish, lionfish

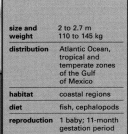

Glossary

Arboreal

Living in the trees.

Balancing pole

Device or organ used to maintain balance and regulate movements.

Brachiation

Method used by certain monkeys to swing by their arms from one creeping plant to another, much like Tarzan.

Bristle

Any thin, thread- or hair-like growth.

Catapult

Ancient weapon used to hurl heavy objects at an enemy.

Cephalopods

Class of molluscs that includes the octopus and the squid.

Crevice

Narrow split or crack of some depth.

Dense

Having a relatively high mass per unit volume.

Earth's magnetic field

Area on the Earth's surface magnetized by the North Pole.

Embryonic

Of or relating to an embryo, the stage of development following the fertilization of the egg.

Feline

Member of the Felidae family of carnivorous mammals, which includes the cat and the tiger.

Habitat

Geographic area in which an animal or plant species lives.

Hydrodynamic

Shaped so as to minimize the resistance of water.

Irrigated

Where blood and other liquids circulate freely and abundantly.

Limestone

Rock made up mainly of calcium carbonate.

Lobe

Rounded, protruding body part (the ear lobe, for example).

Locomotion

Action that allows a living being to move around, to get from one place to another (walking and flying are means of locomotion).

Lustre

Coating that makes a surface shiny and that can serve as protection.

Mammal

Member of any animal species in which the female has mammary glands for feeding her young.

Mangrove

Any tree or shrub found on tropical coats that rests on roots growing above the ground.

Membrane

Thin layer of living cells.

Mucus

Transparent, viscous liquid.

Nutrient

Element providing nourishment that can be assimilated by an organism.

Pectoral

Located on or forming a part of the chest area.

Peduncle

Sort of stem or elongated structure that links two parts of a living being.

Pinion

Portion of a bird's wing that includes the flight feathers.

Prehensile

Capable of grasping and picking things up, even if this is not its primary function.

Reptile

Crawling animal with scale-covered skin, such as the snake, the iguana and the tortoise.

Rudder

Part of a ship that can be moved to change the direction in which the vessel is travelling.

Siphon

Tube that allows water to circulate.

Snaking

Means of locomotion used by animals such as snakes that involves crawling on their ventral surfaces or bellies.

Spinning tube

One of many small tubes from which spiders secrete silk.

Spiral

Rolled in the shape of a winding curve that moves further away from a fixed point with each successive turn.

Sprinter

Runner who specializes in reaching and maintaining top speed over short distances.

Streamlined

Shaped so as to offer minimum resistance; often tapered at both ends like a rocket.

Tube foot

Tube-shaped outgrowth equipped with suckers that protrudes from and can retract into an orifice.

Undulation

Movement of something that rises and falls, like waves.

Valve

Flap-like structure that opens and closes to control the flow of fluid through an organ, pipe, etc.

Webbed

Having fingers connected by a membrane.

Wingspan

Distance between the tips of spread or open wings.

Index

Amphibians

frog 29

Birds

Adelie penguin 7, 29
African jacana 8, 30
Arctic loon 7
Arctic tern 23
common swift 13
diver 29
emperor penguin 29
emu 28
Eurasian nuthatch 11
Eurasian oystercatcher 28
falcons 12
gentoo penguin 28
golden eagle 28
greater roadrunner 19
green-winged teal 28
grouse 12
gulls 12
hawk 28
homing pigeon 28
hummingbirds 12
jacana 9
ostrich 28
penguins 6
peregrine falcon 28
rufous hummingbird 3
spur-winged goose 28
swifts 12
terns 12
tree creepers 10
tundra swan 28
vultures 12
wandering albatross 12, 30
white-throated needletail 28
whooper swan 28
willow ptarmigan 28
woodpeckers 10

Fishes

Atlantic salmon 29
blue shark 28
bluefin tuna 28
common hatchetfish 15
dwarf sea horse 29
eels 6
European eel 23
marlin 28
mudskipper 3
mackerel shark 5, 29
swordfish 5, 28

Insects and other invertebrates

brown snail 29
centipedes 8
common goose barnacle 25
coral 24, 30
crustaceans 8
dragonfly 13, 28
earthworms 20, 21
fanworm 25
five-banded snail 21
flatworms 20
flea 10
flies 10
giant crab 9
grasshopper 29
great green bush-cricket 17
Julid 9
leeches 6, 20
medical leech 21
monarch butterfly 23

pearly nautilus 6, 30
red-spotted crab spider 15
scale insect 25
snails 20
squid 6
starfish 8
water strider 9

Mammals

Atlantic spotted dolphin 4, 30
baird's beaked whale 29
bats 12
black rhinoceros 28
blue wildebeest 22, 30
California sea lion 28
chamois 29
cheetah 18, 19, 28, 30
common dolphin 28
common hippopotamus 2, 3, 30
desert jerboa 17
dolphin 5, 29
domestic dog 29
domestic horse 28, 29
dormice 29
eastern grey kangaroo 3
fin whale 29
flying lemur 15
giant kangaroo 29
giant squirrel 29
giraffe 28
greyhound 28
humans 8
ibex 29
impala 29
killer whale 17, 28, 29
leopard 29
lion 28
Malayan flying lemur 14, 30
martens 10
monkeys 10
opossums 11
prehensile-tailed porcupine 11
Przewalski's horse 19
red deer 28
sea elephant 29
snow leopard 16, 17, 29, 30
spear-nosed bat 13
sperm whale 29
spider monkeys 11
springbok antelope 28, 29
springhare 29
squirrels 10
three-toed sloth 29
tiger 29
timber wolf 28
weddell seal 29
white-handed gibbon 11
white-tailed deer 29
wildebeest 22, 23

Reptiles

bearded dragon 19
black mamba 20, 28, 30
flying dragon 15
galapagos tortoise 29
grey monitor 28
leatherback turtle 5, 28
lizards 10
sea snake 7
snakes 6, 20, 21
tokay gecko 10, 30

A

acrobats 10, 11
Adelie penguin 7, 29
African jacana 8, 30
albatross 13

Arctic loon 7
Arctic tern 23
arms 11
Atlantic salmon 29
Atlantic spotted dolphin 4, 30

B

baird's beaked whale 29
bats 12
bearded dragon 19
birds 4, 8, 12
black mamba 20, 28, 30
black rhinoceros 28
bluefin tuna 28
blue shark 28
blue wildebeest 22, 30
bodies (shape of) 4, 5, 7, 16, 17, 18
bounding 2
brachiation 11
brown snail 29

C

California sea lion 28
centipedes 8
chamois 29
cheetah 18, 19, 28, 30
cilia 6
cirri 25
claws 10, 13, 18
cnidoblasts 24
common dolphin 28
common goose barnacle 25
common hatchetfish 15
common hippopotamus 2, 3, 30
common swift 13
coral 24, 30
crawling 20
crustaceans 8

D

desert jerboa 17
digits 10
diver 29
dolphin 5, 29
domestic dog 29
domestic horse 28, 29
dormice 29
dragonfly 13, 28
dwarf sea horse 29

E

earthworms 20, 21
eastern grey kangaroo 3
eels 6
emperor penguin 29
emu 28
Eurasian nuthatch 11
Eurasian oystercatcher 28
European eel 23

F

falcons 12
fanworm 25
feet 3, 5, 6, 8, 14, 19
fins 3, 4, 6, 15, 17
fin whale 28, 29
fish 4
five-banded snail 21
flatworms 20
flea 29
flies 10
flying 12, 13
flying dragon 15
flying lemur 15

foot 21
frog 29

G

galapagos tortoise 29
gallop 19
gentoo penguin 28
giant crab 9
giant kangaroo 29
giant squirrel 29
giraffe 28
gliding 14
golden eagle 28
grasshopper 29
great green bush-cricket 17
greater roadrunner 19
green-winged teal 28
grey monitor 28
greyhound 28
grouse 12
gulls 12

H

hawk 28
homing pigeon 28
hooves 19
hover 3
humans 8
hummingbirds 12

I

ibex 29
immobility 24, 25
impala 29
insects 6, 8, 12

J

jacana 9
Julid 9

K

killer whale 17, 28, 29

L

leaping 3, 11, 14, 15
leatherback turtle 5, 28
leeches 6, 20
legs 9, 10, 17, 18
leopard 29
lion 28
lizards 10

M

mackerel shark 5, 29
Malayan flying lemur 14, 30
mammals 4
marlin 28
martens 10
medical leech 21
migrations 22
monarch butterfly 23
monkeys 10
mucus 21
mudskipper 3
muscles 3, 4, 15, 16

N

nails 8

O

opossums 11
ostrich 28

P

patagium 14, 15
pearly nautilus 6, 30
penguins 6
peregrine falcon 28
pinions 7
prehensile-tailed porcupine 11
Przewalski's horse 19

R

red deer 28
red-spotted crab spider 15
reptiles 4
rufous hummingbird 3
running 18, 19

S

scale insect 25
sea elephant 29
sea krait (see sea snake)
sea snake 7
sheath 25
siphon 6
skin 4, 5, 13, 14, 15
snails 20
snakes 6, 20, 21
snow leopard 16, 17, 29, 30
spear-nosed bat 13
sperm whale 29
spider monkeys 11
springbok antelope 28, 29
springhare 29
spur-winged goose 28
squid 6
squirrels 10
starfish 8
suckers 10, 21
swifts 12
swimming 4, 5, 6, 7
swordfish 5, 28

T

tail 3, 7, 10, 11, 14, 16, 17, 19
tentacles 25
terns 12
thread 15
three-toed sloth 29
tiger 29
timber wolf 28
toes 8, 11
tokay gecko 10, 30
tree creepers 10
tundra swan 28

U

undulations 4, 6, 7

V

vultures 12

W

walking 8, 9, 10
wandering albatross 12, 30
water 4
water strider 9
webbed feet 2, 6, 7
weddell seal 29
white-handed gibbon 11
white-tailed deer 29
white-throated needletail 28
whooper swan 28
wildebeest 22, 23
willow ptarmigan 28
wings 6, 12, 13, 19
woodpeckers 10

32

The terms in **bold characters** refer to an illustration; those in *italics* indicate a keyword.

So Many Ways to Get Around was created and produced by **QA International**, a division of Les Éditions Québec Amérique inc, 329, rue de la Commune Ouest, 3ᵉ étage, Montréal (Québec) H2Y 2E1 Canada **T** 514.499.3000 **F** 514.499.3010
©1999 Éditions Québec Amérique inc.

ISBN 2-89037-980-9

Printed and bound in Canada

10 9 8 7 6 5 4 3 2 1   99